BEDOUIN

Stella Peters

Macdonald Educational

Editor Caroline Sheldrick
Design Roland Blunk MSIAD
Picture Research Jenny Golden
Production Rosemary Bishop

First published 1980

Macdonald Educational Ltd
Holywell House
Worship Street
London EC2A 2EN

© Macdonald Educational 1980

ISBN 0 356 05955 3

Made and printed by
Waterlow (Dunstable) Limited
England

Artists
Key: T top; B bottom; L left; R right;
C centre.
Terry Allen Designs: 31(B)
Moira Chesmur: 4–5, 16–17
Hayward Art Group: 7(T), 7(B),
11(T), 11(R), 15(TR), 15(TL), 21(T),
22–23, 27, 37(T)
Tony Payne: 19(T), 28
Pat Elliot Shircore: 44–45

Contents

The desert and its people

"The strength of the Bedouin lies in their constant movement."
Arab proverb

A vast area of desert stretches from the Arabian peninsula in the east to the west coast of North Africa. It is broken only by the Red Sea and the Nile valley. At its core is a hot, wind-swept waste where no rain falls. No life is possible except in rare oases, where water wells up from far below the ground. Desert travellers rely on these for their survival.

Around this barren area are semi-deserts where some rain falls in the winter. A few plants survive even in the long, hot summers. Here there is just enough food to provide a bare living for small numbers of people and animals. Camels, sheep and goats are the domestic animals best suited to these conditions.

The Bedouin character

The people who lived in these harsh lands were called Bedouin, from the Arabic word *Badawi* (plural *Badu*) meaning "nomads" or "wanderers." They were tough and fearless, and fiercely loyal to their own tribal groups. They bravely defended their homeland against intruders, but were generous and hospitable to any strangers who came in peace to find shelter, rest, food and safety.

Their pattern of life

They lived in a way which made the most of their difficult surroundings. They were wandering herdsmen owning camels, sheep and goats, for whose sake they were constantly in search of fresh pastures, especially in the spring months.

The *Badu* were intensely proud of their hardiness, and poured scorn on those people who had settled in the more fertile lands near the coast. "They eat watermelons," one Bedouin said of them, "and grow big-bellied and soft."

Here is part of a Bedouin camp of Libya setting out for a new location. The sheikh or headman will have gone ahead to choose the site. The flocks and herds with their herdsmen will be following behind at a more leisurely pace, grazing as they go.

Camels carry the rolled-up tents, and smaller household items are held in nets hanging like panniers at their sides. Sometimes lambs and kids travel in the nets. The mother and child ride in a special canopy, left uncovered in this case because the day is pleasant.

Outriders keep the camel train in line.

The spread of Islam

"The Hilal tribe poured into Africa like a swarm of locusts, pillaging and destroying everything they found in their path."
Arab historian Ibn Khaloun (1332–1406) about the Bedouin invasion of Africa

The nomadic way of life is an ancient one. The Bible tells how Abraham and his family and descendants lived in tents in the Negeb (Negev) desert, and owned flocks and herds. Over 3,000 years ago Moses and the children of Israel were wanderers in the Sinai desert after their exodus from Egypt.

The true Bedouin
The true Bedouin came from the Arabian peninsula. Until nearly 600 years after the birth of Christ, they remained pagans, worshipping many gods in the form of idols and sacred stones. The most sacred was the Black Stone which was kept at Mecca.

Mohammad and the rise of Islam
A boy was born in Mecca in about AD 570, named Mohammad. He became convinced that there was only one god and that he, Mohammad, had been chosen to proclaim Him to the Arabs. He named his new religion *Islam* ("peace").

The citizens of Mecca were hostile to Mohammad, and so he moved with his family and friends to another town, Madinah (now Medina). Here he converted not only the townspeople, but also the surrounding Bedouin tribes. Under his leadership they formed an army which first captured Mecca and then spread Islam throughout Arabia.

After Mohammad's death in AD 632, his followers left Arabia, carrying their faith and language with them. Eventually the Islamic empire stretched from Spain and southern France to the borders of China.

At this time they occupied only the coastal areas of North Africa, leaving the desert to the Berbers. In the 11th century another invasion of Bedouin drove the Berbers west to modern Libya, occupying the land themselves.

6

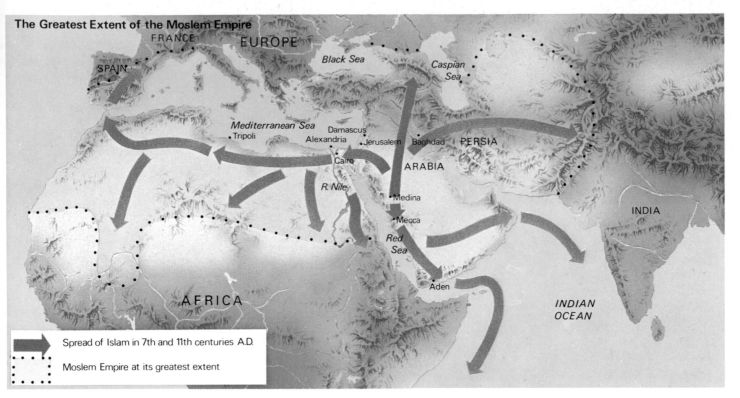

The Greatest Extent of the Moslem Empire

FRANCE
EUROPE
SPAIN
Black Sea
Caspian Sea
Mediterranean Sea
Tripoli
Damascus
Alexandria
Jerusalem
Baghdad
PERSIA
ARABIA
Cairo
R. Nile
Medina
INDIA
Mecca
Red Sea
AFRICA
Aden
INDIAN OCEAN

➔ Spread of Islam in 7th and 11th centuries A.D.

⋯ Moslem Empire at its greatest extent

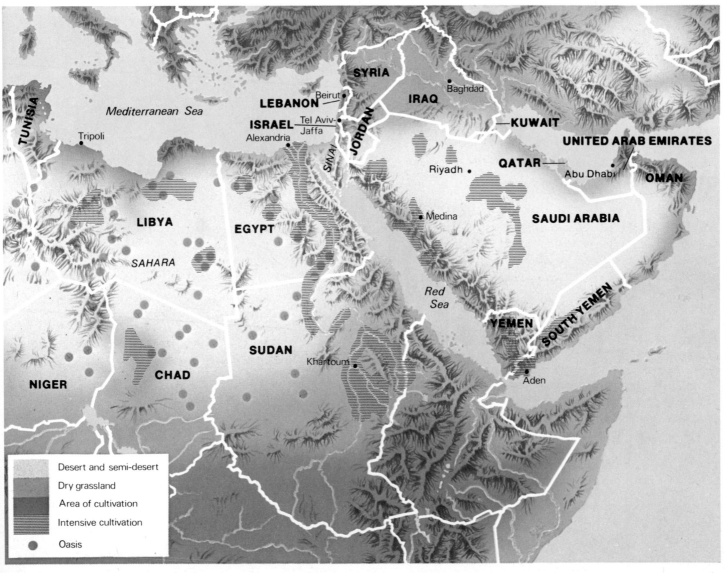

TUNISIA
Mediterranean Sea
SYRIA
LEBANON — Beirut
Baghdad
IRAQ
ISRAEL — Tel Aviv- Jaffa
Tripoli
Alexandria
SINAI
JORDAN
KUWAIT
UNITED ARAB EMIRATES
QATAR
Riyadh
Abu Dhabi
OMAN
LIBYA
EGYPT
Medina
SAUDI ARABIA
SAHARA
Red Sea
SUDAN
Khartoum
YEMEN
SOUTH YEMEN
NIGER
CHAD
Aden

Desert and semi-desert
Dry grassland
Area of cultivation
Intensive cultivation
● Oasis

The changing seasons

"O mother of rain! rain upon us! From God's measure, measure out to us. O mother of rain! rain upon us; a real flood let our share be."
Women of the Rwala tribe; part of a prayer for rain

As with all people who live close to nature, the Bedouin way of life was determined by the changing seasons.

In summer, the desert shimmers with intense heat. The sun's rays beat down from a clear sky and the temperature at noon soars to 50°C. Scorching winds frequently blow from the heart of the desert, bringing dust and sandstorms. Such heat can only be endured because the air is very dry; after sunset the temperature falls rapidly and the nights are cool.

The coming of the rain
The rain falls in winter, but it is extremely unreliable, and many areas may have little or none at all.

If the rains were late, the Bedouin became very anxious. They would scan the sky for clouds, and ask all who came to their camps, "Has rain come to you yet?" Many were the prayers for rain at this time.

When rain falls, it is often heavy, accompanied by violent thunderstorms. It floods the ground, turning the river valleys *(wadis)* into roaring torrents, and fills to the brim all the underground cisterns from which the Bedouin drew their water.

The miracle of spring
As soon as the first rains fall, millions of seeds, which were lying dormant in the dry earth, suddenly spring into growth. In a few days, a fresh green haze covers the ground, and in a week or two the desert is carpeted with flowers. Irises, crocuses, marigolds, buttercups, daisies and asphodels make a riot of colour. Wild thymes and other aromatic plants fill the air with fragrance when crushed underfoot.

Spring for the Bedouin was the happiest time of year; the animals had plenty to eat, and the milk flowed.

8

Below: Goats being watered. In spring, the flocks obtain enough moisture from the fresh green plants they eat, and do not need to drink. In summer when the plants have gone they must be driven to permanent wells, or have water brought to them in barrels.

Bottom of page: A shepherd boy with his flock of sheep grazing on the green herbage in a *wadi* in Saudi Arabia. The green cover is very thin, and quickly becomes exhausted, so the flock must be constantly moved to find new pastures.

Flocks and herds

"The Bedouin measure their wealth first by the number of their sons, next by their camels, next by their sheep, and finally by their goats."
Sheikh Yusaf of Libya

Below: Bedouin girls in Jordan using donkeys to bring water from a well. The water is poured into large leather bags hanging from wooden supports which rest on the donkey's back. Funnels are used for getting the water into the necks of the bags.

Bottom of page: Syrian women milking sheep. When the sheep are ready for milking, they are lined up, each one facing the opposite direction from the next, and their heads tied together by ropes round their necks. Two women usually milk the line, one on each side.

Without camels the Bedouin could not have lived in the desert at all. The camel survives the summer drought because when it drinks it can store enough water in its stomach to last for up to fifteen days. It has reserves of fat in its hump so that it can go for several days without food; it is able to eat the dry, leathery and thorny shrubs which are the only plants that survive in summer. Its large, flat feet can move easily over the desert sands and gravels, and its great strength enables it to carry heavy loads.

Sheep and goats

Some tribes in the Arabian desert herded only camels, but the Bedouin of North Africa, Sinai and the Negev owned sheep and goats as well. They yielded wool and hair for weaving and plentiful supplies of milk in spring. They were slaughtered for meat, but only on special occasions – weddings, funerals, religious feasts and to welcome important guests. They were given as gifts, and could be sold.

Horses, donkeys and dogs

Horses were highly prized and much cherished. They needed watering twice a day, had to be fed on grain throughout the year, and in summer had to shelter from the sun inside the tents. Horses were expensive and so were their saddles and bridles, beautifully embroidered with silver thread; only the wealthy owned them.

Donkeys were used for riding by poor men, and carried water from the wells and other light loads.

All camps had their watchdogs, the semi-wild *pariah* or *pie* dogs. Their barking, particularly at night, warned of the approach of strangers or of wild animals. Shepherds took them to guard the flocks at night from the ravages of wolves, hyenas and jackals.

Camel saddles

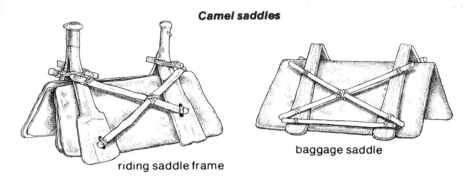

riding saddle frame

baggage saddle

Left: Camel saddles are made so that they fit over the animal's hump. They have a wooden framework, but this must be well padded on the underside so that the camel's skin is not chafed by the wood. When placed in position over the hump, and held by ropes running underneath the body, the saddle cannot slip forwards or backwards. Riding saddles have high pommels before and behind and are well padded above with sheepskins and blankets to make sitting more comfortable.

Pack saddles have no pommel.

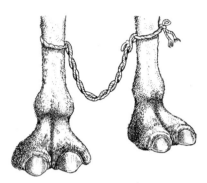

Above: Straying camels are always a problem for the Bedouin. When not being used, the camel was left to browse the desert plants. To stop it wandering too far, it was hobbled by having its front legs tied together.

Below: So that a rider could mount easily, or so that it could be loaded up, the camel was made to kneel on the ground. It could be forced to remain in this position by having a hobbling rope tied round one of its bended front knees.

Left: Camel herd in Arabia. The camel used by the Bedouin is the one-humped camel or dromedary – not the two-humped bactrian camel used in central Asia. It has been called "the ship of the desert" since no other animal is capable of travelling long distances in desert conditions, usually carrying heavy burdens.

Cultivation

"Za, za, a wedding canopy (for you) and a pair of dark eyes (for me)!"

With these words a young man would urge on his ploughing camel. The "dark eyes" were those of his dream bride

Below: Crops in a Saudi Arabian valley. This is an area of intense cultivation in an oasis. The crops are watered by irrigation, each cultivated bed being surrounded by a channel through which water runs. The crops are raised by settled people living in the oasis but the Bedouin migrate there in summer and, when the crops have been harvested, they graze sheep on the stubble. This is a very useful addition to the natural pasture which by that time is exhausted. The Bedouin can obtain food for themselves as well, selling camels or camel hair to pay.

Camel herders in the Arabian desert cultivated no crops. Their chief food was camels' milk, but they needed wheat to supplement their diet. This they obtained from farmers *(fellahin)* in the oases and coastal areas. They believed this grain was theirs by right, and if the farmers would not willingly give it, it could be taken by force.

Farming the desert
In the Sahara, Sinai and Negev deserts, whenever rainfall was sufficient, the Bedouin grew their own crops of wheat and barley.

At the onset of the rainy season, scouts went out on camels and searched their tribal territory for a suitable rain-soaked place. When one was found, word was sent back to the camp, and every able-bodied man went there with his plough and his gun. Sometimes, if the wet area was on the border of two territories, disputes and skirmishes arose over whose right it was to plough there.

Growing and storing grain
First the seed was scattered over the wet ground, and then ploughed in. Then the crop was left until harvest time. There were no fences put up, so if a shepherd or camel herd passed that way it was his duty to keep his animals off it. At harvest time, the men returned to cut, thresh and winnow the crop. Because different areas were ploughed every year, the soil never became exhausted. If enough rain fell, and there was a bumper crop, the surplus could be stored in case of a drought. Shallow pits were dug and lined with straw, then the grain was piled in to form a mound which was covered with straw and then wetted clay, which dried firm. In such mounds the grain was safe from rotting for about five years.

Below left: A Bedouin farmer and his wife winnowing wheat in Jordan. The grain is piled into a mound, and the farmer tosses it up in the air using a long-handled pitchfork. The heavy grain falls to the ground and the light chaff is carried away by the wind.

Below: A young man using a camel to pull his plough in Libya. The grain is first broadcast over land which has been wetted by rain, and it is afterwards ploughed in. The simple wooden plough with its metal "shoe" does no more than scratch the ground surface.

Below left: Man filling a sack with wheat at a grain store in Libya. One of the storage mounds has been opened, and the sack is being filled to take back to the camp for grinding. The caretaker of the store measures out the grain.

Below: Bunches of dates hanging from a palm tree at an oasis in eastern Arabia. Dates form an essential part of the Bedouin diet. In Libya where oases are few and deep in the desert interior, young men made hazardous journeys of hundreds of kilometres to bring back supplies to the camps.

The tent

"O new tent we raise you, may you be filled with children and happiness."
"The camels will carry you, your blessing will increase, Children will play in you, men will salute you, God will sustain you."
Songs sung by women when erecting a new tent (Cyrenaica)

People always on the move must have a portable dwelling. The Bedouin tents were ideal for their way of life. They were easy to erect and dismantle; they could keep out even the heaviest winter rains and give shade from the scorching summer sun.

Black tents and white tents

All Bedouin tents had the same basic shape and construction, but the goat-hair tents of Arabia were black, and the Saharan tents were white. The white tents were made from sheep's wool and white goat's hair, with distinctive black panels along each side, and decorative brown edges. The wool expanded when wet and so kept rain out. A new tent of this type was so cherished that it was taken down in summer and replaced by an older tent, no longer waterproof, and patched all over in cotton. These cotton pieces were usually pink or blue.

Making a tent

The camel herders of Arabia had no source of sheep or goat hair so they bought their tents in the towns. Among the sheep and goat herders, the women took great pride in weaving their own.

The tent top was made up of six or eight long woven strips sewn together to form a rectangle. It was supported by two main poles, or more, depending on its length. The corners and sides were supported by shorter poles, and the whole was held up by guy ropes held by pegs. Four loose tent walls were pinned to the top.

The women did all the work connected with the tents. They made them, put them up and took them down, and rushed out on wet nights to adjust the ropes; otherwise they might snap, or pull out the pegs making the tent collapse.

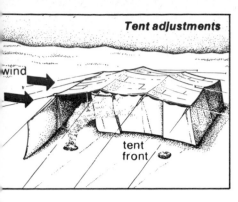

Tent adjustments

wind

tent front

Far left: A Libyan tent being pitched. See how different its colour is from the black tent.

Left: A tent adjusted for wind direction. The fire is shielded and the smoke blown away from the entrance.

Right: A top view of a Libyan tent showing how it is made up of different coloured woven strips sewn together.

Below: A Bedouin tent in the desert of Judaea, Israel. Black tents like this are found all over Arabia. Stones are used to weigh down the tent pegs and the side curtains.

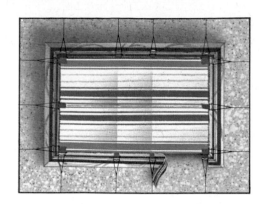

Inside the tent

Whenever strangers approached, a long, brightly coloured curtain was hung up right across the tent from back to front, suspended in the centre from one of the main poles, making two "rooms". In a two-pole tent, these would be of unequal sizes; the male guests were entertained by the host and his sons in the larger side.

Women's side

The men did not intrude into the other side. The younger women and girls stayed out of sight behind the curtain, listening avidly to what was said, and peeping over whenever they thought they wouldn't be noticed.

This side contained all the utensils for food preparation and cooking: the grindstones, cauldrons and wooden bowls. Women rarely sat idle; when they were not busy with other tasks they spun wool on their spindles.

There were straw mats on the earth, often with sheepskins for sitting on, and a row of storage sacks for grain or dates, covered by a coloured woven carpet. A wooden chest held the best clothes and other treasures.

The men's part was made beautiful with coloured carpets on the straw mats. The men rested their backs against the storage sacks which were covered with the best carpets. Camel saddles would be on this side, and if the host owned a horse, its saddle would have pride of place.

Fireplaces

In Arabian tents, there was a hollowed-out fireplace in the centre of the men's part, round which they sat on winter's nights and where coffee was made. In the Sahara, a small container of glowing embers would be brought in and placed on a bare patch of earth when tea was about to be brewed.

A Libyan tent with the dividing curtain in place. The men leave their shoes outside so they do not spoil the carpets laid out for them. They have been drinking tea, and the boys have not yet taken away the equipment. This consists of a brass tray holding tea glasses and a teapot, a kettle, and a box containing the embers of a fire on which the tea is boiled.

It may look odd to see a petrol can on the women's side. Many were in fact left lying in the desert after World War II, and the Bedouin use them as water containers.

Weaving

Right: Women express their creativity and love of colour in weaving carpets, saddle bags and curtains. The patterns are learned by daughters as they watch their mothers at work. The men do no art work of any kind, though long ago they were renowned as poets and storytellers.

Below: A woman in Qatar weaving in her tent. Bedouin looms were very simple, consisting of just a few short poles and two flat pieces of wood like swords.

All Bedouin women learned to weave because they had to be able to make tent strips. Black tent strips were plain. They had very hard wear and suffered the ravages of rain, wind and sun, so they were replaced often. Decorating them would hardly have been worthwhile. In the Sahara the tent strips were decorated, but only with the easy lengthwise designs and only with the different natural colours of the wool and hair.

Decorated work

When it came to weaving dividing curtains for the tents, carpets, cushion covers, saddle bags and nose bags, then the women could really give their creative imagination full rein.

Some of the wool was dyed in bright colours: red, deep blue, yellow and green. Patterns were made running across the weaving in chevrons, triangles, diamonds and zigzags. Sometimes multi-coloured pompoms were put in and the ends finished with plaits and tassels. From infancy little girls watched their mothers weaving and soon learned the art of making these patterns.

At the loom

Weaving was done in the summer when the flocks and herds were away from the camps, so that the looms were not trampled on. The women had more time, without the milking and the butter and cheese to make. Also there was little danger of rainfall which could make the colours run. The dyes sold in the markets were of poor quality and ran easily.

The loom was usually set up so that the women working sat inside the tent in the shade while the other end stretched out into the open. As the work grew, the woven part was rolled up and the other end brought in.

Bedouin weaving

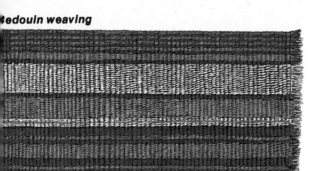

carpet

camel trapping

bag

Growing up

"Satan, by day, lives in the heads of the little boys; By night, in the heads of the dogs."
Bedouin proverb – said as a joke by a fond father

Below: A young girl herding goats in Qatar. She has not yet reached the age for marriage, so she can go freely without having to hide her face. This is a part of the Arab world where many women wear masks.

Bottom of page: Boys from Saudi Arabia riding a donkey. It was every boy's ambition to own a horse when he became a man, though few were able to achieve their aim. Most had to be content with donkeys unless they were making long journeys on camelback.

Bedouin children were well loved; many died in infancy so those who survived were doubly precious. When a boy was born, there was a great feast for all friends and relations, who came with gifts. There was a feast for a girl, too, but without meat.

Young children had their hair shaved and their faces left dirty; it was feared that if they looked too beautiful an envious person would put the "Evil Eye" on them.

Circumcision

The major event of a small boy's life was his circumcision, which took place when he was about five. There was a great feast, with meat. Men fired their rifles and women "trilled" with their tongues.

For a girl, there was a lesser special occasion, when her face was tattooed. There was another meatless feast.

Growing up

Up to the age of 11 or 12, the boys and girls ran freely together. They ran errands between the tents, helped bring water from the wells, collected camel dung for fuel, and in the spring looked after the kids and lambs. They had no schools and never learned to read or write.

As the girls grew more mature they wore shawls over their heads which they could pull over their faces to hide them. They helped their mothers inside the tent, especially with cooking and weaving.

The boys grew to respect and obey their fathers and fathers' brothers. They would never tell jokes in front of them, particularly jokes about girls! Youths began to do men's work which took them further away from the camps: shepherding, camel herding, bringing dates from oases, goat herding and taking part in raids.

Left: Children drawing up water from a well in Libya with a patient donkey waiting to carry it back to the camp.

Right: A baby in a cradle specially designed with rope straps which the mother could put her arms through, for carrying it on her back. It could also be suspended from the tent roof.

Below: A group of poor Bedouin children trying to make a little money for themselves by offering quartz for sale to tourists in the Sinai desert.

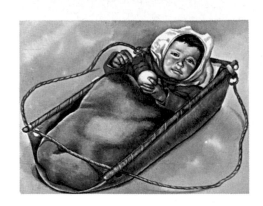

Marriage

"There are those who are cheap for two hundred camels, And there are those who are expensive for the skin of a young camel."
Part of a Bedouin rhyme about wives

Below: The bridal camel with the wedding canopy on its back waiting outside the tent where the bride is being adorned.

A young man stands nearby with his rifle ready so that he can fire it in her honour when she comes out.

Bottom of page: The bride inside the canopy, hidden by a coloured blanket. Two young men have stopped the camel by kneeling in its path. They have sung a song to her and are now firing their rifles in her honour. The women wait to form a procession behind.

Bedouin marriages were arranged. Sometimes the bride and groom had never met each other before the wedding day.

Marriages between first cousins, the children of brothers, were very common. A man had the right to claim his father's brother's daughter and his permission was gained before she married anyone else. Many girls preferred this kind of marriage, because they knew their cousins, having grown up with them. They would continue to live in the same camp near their mothers and sisters, and their husbands could not ill-treat them with their fathers and brothers close by.

Bridal gifts

Before the wedding a settlement was made; the groom's father promised to give the bride's father an agreed number of camels. The bride was given a trousseau of new clothes, carpets, blankets and other household goods, and jewellery, particularly two heavy silver bracelets.

Marriage failure

Sometimes marriages failed, usually because there were no sons. This was seen as a failing in the wife. Her husband might then divorce her and marry someone else. If he was wealthy and did not wish to part with her, he might marry a second wife; up to four were allowed. Each wife must have her own tent and the husband must spend alternate days and nights in each. Few Bedouin had two wives; hardly any had more.

Divorce was easy for a man. All he needed to do was to say "I divorce you" to his wife, three times. All a woman could do if she wanted her freedom was return to her father and wait until her husband divorced her.

Below: Male guests gathered for a Bedouin wedding in Abu Dhabi. They are sitting in an enclosure made with palm fronds brought from a nearby oasis. These give shade while allowing free circulation of the air.

Bottom of page: As the shadows lengthen, the dancing begins. A girl, with her face completely veiled, comes forward to dance. The young men gather round her in a semicircle, singing and clapping and she faces them, shaking her hips in rhythm and waving a cane over their heads.

Saharan wedding

If the bride lives in a different camp, a party of young men, the groom's brothers and cousins, go to fetch her. They are mounted on gaily decked horses and camels and wear their best clothes. With her comes a woman relative, usually her aunt.

Preparing the bride

On the wedding morning, the bride is dressed in her new clothes and jewellery, her eyes outlined in black khol, and her hands and feet dyed red with henna. She is completely covered by a shawl and led to her bridal camel. She mounts and sits inside the wedding canopy completely hidden from view. Sometimes a small boy is put in with her "so that she may have sons". Only women take part in preparing the bride. A woman takes the camel's rein and leads it through the camp towards the wedding tent, all singing and "trilling" with their tongues. The wedding tent is pitched a little way from the camp and here the bridegroom is waiting with his friends.

The wedding tent

When the procession arrives, the camel is led seven times round the tent before the bride dismounts and slips into a curtained-off part within. The bridegroom goes in to see her there, but no one else may enter except her woman relative. There follows a wedding feast for which several lambs and kids have been killed.

The groom's father and other elders of the camp stay away from the proceedings to avoid embarrassing the young people who may never sing love songs or even mention weddings in front of their fathers.

The wedding celebrations will go on for seven days.

23

Adult life

"A man between two women is like a lamb between two wolves."
Bedouin proverb explaining why most Bedouin have only one wife

"The woman is to the man as the tentpole is to the tent."
Bedouin proverb

In the everyday life of a Bedouin camp, men and women each had their own work. Never did one do the work of the other. Only the bringing of water from the well was done by both. The women went to the wells nearby with donkeys and small water containers for daily supplies. The men took camels to large, distant wells to fill much bigger tanks.

Men and women at work

Men gave the women wool and hair for weaving, and made the tent ropes from halfa grass. Apart from that, the women did all the work connected with the tent. The men might help with the heavy main tent poles, but nothing else.

The men provided the grain, the animals, goods from the towns and dates from the oases, but the women prepared all the food. They milked the animals, made butter and cheese, ground grain and made bread and other cereal dishes. They also collected the brushwood for the fire, helped by the children.

The men made the coffee or tea for their male guests, but apart from that did no cooking of any kind. The women looked after the small children and did the washing.

Time for raiding

Many men did little or no work of the kind described. Herding required few men and these could be the younger sons of the family, or hired hands. Sowing, ploughing and harvesting were hard work, but did not take long. Besides, in the old days wealthy men owned slaves. So many men had time for warfare, raiding and hunting. They attended tribal disputes which needed long meetings, and there was much argument before a settlement was reached.

Below: Bedouin men watering camels at a well. They draw up the water in a leather bucket and pour it into a special drinking trough made of wood and camel skin. It is also their duty to clean out the wells to prevent them from becoming blocked by sand and silt.

Bottom of page: Jordanian women, helped by children, pinning a new tent side onto the top. The pitching and striking of tents and all the adjustments for weather are done entirely by them. The only part men might play is in the handling of the heavy main tent poles.

Right: A most unexpected sight from the Libyan desert – men at work sewing up a woman's dress!

Below: The market at Beersheba, a town in Israel, where Bedouin men come to shop. The goods on display are embroidered dresses and rolls of cloth. One man is fingering the cloth to test its quality. The stallholders are mostly men. The women present are townswomen.

Preparing food

Below: Part of the market in Riyadh, the capital city of Saudi Arabia. For centuries Bedouin tribes from the surrounding deserts came here for supplies. In the background is a mosque, the building in which Moslems gather to pray, with its tall minaret from which the call to prayer is made.

The stalls display a variety of fresh fruits for sale, but most Bedouin could not afford them, and they would be too perishable to take back into the desert. Dates were the fruit eaten by all Bedouin. Many camel herders existed for most of the year on dates and milk.

Even wealthy Bedouin ate little most of the time, and the poor seldom had enough to eat. Foodstuffs had to be easily carried, and able to withstand great heat. Except in spring, their diet was monotonous.

Cereals, especially wheat, were their basic food. They ate some of the grain roasted or boiled, but most was ground into flour for bread or for dumplings boiled in broth. They enjoyed rice on special occasions, and ate lots of dates. Clarified butter was mixed with everything.

Nothing wasted

Animals were only killed for special feasts. Even then, every bit was used. They ate the liver and flesh at once and cracked the bones to suck out the marrow. Other parts, like the stomach and intestines, were dried on the tent roof for making broth later.

Men hunted wild animals and women collected wild plants for extra food, flavourings and medicines.

The fire was lit in a shallow pit just outside the tent entrance, and the cooking pot was put over it on three stones.

Eating apart

Men and women never ate together. Father and sons ate on one side of the dividing curtain and mother and daughters on the other.

All those eating together sat round one large bowl and scooped up the food with their right hands. Hand washing before and after the meal was an important ritual, though only a few drops of precious water were used.

Coffee was the favourite drink in Arabia. Islam forbids the drinking of alcohol, but the bitter, milkless coffee made an excellent stimulant. In the Sahara they drank very strong, sweet, milkless tea instead.

Grinding wheat

A Libyan woman grinding wheat, using a pair of round grindstones. The top one has a wooden handle which she holds with her right hand, rotating one stone on the other. With her left, she takes handfuls of grain from the basket, and drops them into the central hole. The flour comes out from between the stones and falls onto an upturned sheepskin.

Only enough flour is ground for each day's needs. While she turns, she chants a rhythmical song. Some wealthy families had grain milled for them in the towns.

Making bread

Jordanian women making one kind of bread. The dough was mixed from flour and water with a little salt, but no yeast. It was broken into small pieces, and each piece was patted between the hands until it became thin and flat, like a large pancake. This was flapped onto the metal dome raised on stones over the fire, and was cooked in seconds.

In Libya the dough was made into small round loaves which were baked in an earth oven, simply a hole in the ground in which a fire had been lit and allowed to die down.

Milking the animals

A Jordanian woman milking a goat. Spring was the time when the goats and sheep had their young, and yielded milk. The milking was done in the evening when the flocks returned from the pastures. Some of the fresh milk was drunk immediately, particularly by the children, and the rest was first warmed, then poured into goatskin bags in which it soon turned sour. One of the joys of spring for the goat and sheep herders was the plentiful supply of this sour milk for drinking.

Churning butter

A Jordanian woman making butter. Some of the sour milk was churned in a blown-up goatskin bag to produce butter. In Libya the woman held the bag in her hands and shook it from side to side, a laborious task, but in Arabia the bag was hung on a wooden tripod and shaken to and fro with one hand only, leaving the other free. Rhythmical songs were often chanted during churning.

When the butter formed, it was clarified by boiling. Camel milk was not suitable for butter-making, being without cream.

Making cheese

Cheese could be made from goat, sheep or camel milk and was easily portable. It was carried by travellers crossing the desert, and by shepherds away with their flocks.

The sour milk was first boiled, then strained in a fabric bag so that the water drained away. The remaining curd was kneaded with some salt until it hardened, then it was shaped into small round cheeses which were dried in the sun on the tent top.

They could be eaten hard, or pounded up and mixed with water, then drunk.

Hunting and wild animals

Hunting was a favourite pastime of Bedouin men. Every boy grew up able to track animals in the sand, a skill essential to a good hunter.

Two kinds of animals were hunted: the animals which preyed on the flocks and herds, like wolves, jackals and hyenas, panthers, cheetahs and leopards; and those whose meat made a very useful supplement to the diet. There were several kinds of antelopes, addax, oryx, ibex and gazelle, as well as smaller animals like jerboas.

Hunting on a camel

Traditional means of hunting were often long and arduous. The hunter might stalk his quarry for days before catching up with it if he was on foot.

If he rode a camel, he would dismount when some distance from the prey, and approach, using the camel as a screen, until he was close enough to shoot. Bringing back an oryx became a great mark of distinction in Arabia.

Many hunters kept saluki dogs, speedy animals like greyhounds. They would chase the larger animals until they exhausted them and then hold them at bay until the hunter came up.

Gazelles were so fast they could often outrun the salukis, so only the young or lame ones were caught.

Hunting with falcons

Falconry was, and still is, very popular, particularly among the wealthy. Falcons and salukis were used together to hunt small game such as hares and foxes, and game birds like bustards, partridges and quail. The dogs roved the hunting grounds starting up the prey and then the falcons were released to catch it. It was said that a well-trained falcon could catch ten bustards and twenty hares in one day if game was plentiful.

Below: Some of the wild animals of desert lands (*not drawn to scale*). The oryx, addax and gazelle were hunted by the poorer Bedouin for their meat, and by the wealthy for sport. Many are now almost extinct in the wild.

Game birds, like the lesser bustard, were also hunted, and many smaller animals like jerboas, hares and even large lizards and locusts were caught and eaten by the poor. Hyenas, wolves and jackals preyed on the flocks. Poisonous snakes and scorpions were killed whenever they were found.

Desert animals not to scale

striped hyena

oryx

Dorcas gazelle

addax

jerboa

puff adder

black scorpion

little bustard

Left: The saluki dog is a kind of greyhound used for hunting in Arabia. It is extremely fast and can easily run down hares and gazelle. Salukis and hawks were often used together in gazelle hunting. Unlike common camp dogs, salukis were allowed inside the tents.

Below: A falcon being trained in Dubai. Hawking and falconry were popular in Arabia from early times. The Bedouin snared the wild birds using nets baited with live jerboas or pigeons, then tamed and trained them. They were used for hunting lesser bustard and even gazelle.

Bedouin out hunting would sometimes kill a mother gazelle which was with her young one. They would take the baby back to camp and find a goat which would act as a foster mother, preferably one which had lost its own kid. The gazelle would drink the goat's milk until it was old enough to be taken to market and sold, by which time it would be quite tame.

Preserving the herds

Nowadays animals like the oryx and the gazelle are captured for another reason. There has been mass slaughter of these animals by hunters in cars and even aeroplanes, using rifles and machine guns. Naturalists have become concerned for their survival. Operation Oryx, launched in 1972, takes wild animals into captivity to build up breeding herds and later re-introduce them into their natural habitats.

Oryx as unicorns

Wild animals have been kept in captivity in Arab lands for centuries. In 1503 an Italian travelled to Mecca disguised as a soldier guarding a pilgrim caravan from marauding Bedouin. He told an intriguing tale of seeing two unicorns in the Great Mosque. Stories of these legendary creatures were widespread in medieval times. From his description, they seemed to be more like antelopes than horses, but having a single horn in the centre of the forehead. It has been suggested that the animals were really oryx which had lost one horn in youth. The Italian said they were a gift from the King of Ethiopia and were shown to the people "as a miracle".

Gazelles were kept in the households of wealthy town Arabs, as pets for the women and children.

Bedouin clothing

Below: A Libyan Bedouin in full dress. In camp he would wear a long, white cotton shirt and trousers, and a white cotton skullcap, with perhaps a strip of cotton wound to form a turban.

On special occasions, he would wear a red felt hat over the skullcap, a coloured waistcoat and, over all, a long piece of woollen material or *jerd*, which he draped round his body, pulling it up over his head when he needed extra protection. His wife wears a long cotton dress sashed with a woollen band. Over her head is a black cotton scarf.

Bedouin clothing had to suit the desert conditions. In spite of the summer heat, they wore clothes which covered them from head to foot. They could not expose their light-coloured skins to the burning sun. Their garments were loose and flowing, with wide sleeves, so that air could circulate freely underneath. The perspiration evaporated and cooled the skin.

When the temperatures dropped sharply at night and on wet winter days, they needed extra coverings to put on. The chance of desert sandstorms made it essential that travellers' head coverings could be pulled right over their faces to prevent sand from filling their eyes, ears, nostrils and mouths.

Fabrics and colours

Most of their clothes were made of cotton, which is cool, with wraps of wool for extra warmth. Some even wore sheepskin coats in winter. Silk was only for the wealthy.

As for colour, the men's basic garments were white, while women wore many colours – flowery prints in reds, pinks and blues, or black embroidered with coloured threads. All clothes and materials for making them were bought by the men when they went to market.

Veils and masks

Moslem townswomen in the past were completely veiled when they went out, or wore elaborate masks to hide their features; many still do. Bedouin women were always much freer, and in many areas did not cover their faces at all. Young girls, however, would turn modestly away from the public gaze. Along the Persian Gulf, in Kuwait, Oman and Qatar, and also in Sinai, they often did wear masks.

Right: Bedouin women loved jewellery. A bridegroom's father agreed to give jewellery to his son's wife; especially a pair of heavy silver bracelets.

Necklaces of beads spaced with silver charms, large silver hoop earrings and nose rings were widely worn. Also there were little silver boxes containing some words from the Koran; these were hung on chains.

Nearly all Bedouin jewellery was made of silver; only the wealthy could afford gold.

Married women wore scented necklaces made from perfumed plant material.

Below: A Jordanian Bedouin woman. Like her Libyan "sister" she has no covering on her face and her tattoo marks show up well. These were common throughout the area for town and Bedouin women and were thought to enhance their beauty.

Bottom of page: Bedouin from Arabia. The outer garment worn here is a long sleeveless woollen coat without fastening, called an *abba*, usually black or dark brown in colour. The head covering is a camel hair cap with a white and red kerchief on top. It was held in place by a double band of black cord.

31

Tribe, sheikh and camp

Below: A meeting between two rival Bedouin groups in Libya. They were disputing the ownership of a well. Prominent sheikhs from several other groups were there by invitation, to act as go-betweens.

They sat in the shade of a carob tree, and began by reciting the first words of the Koran.

Bottom of page: A small spring camp in the hills of Samaria, Israel. The tents are pitched where there is fresh green pasture for the flocks to graze on. They remain nearby for milking and so that the young lambs and kids can be protected inside the tents at night.

All Bedouin belonged to tribes. Each tribe claimed descent from a common ancestor, and many Bedouin could recite long pedigrees to prove it.

The tribe was divided into smaller groups. Of these, the most important was the "kin group" of five generations of men. It included a man, his father and his grandfather, and his sons and grandsons. Also included were his uncles (father's brothers), his cousins (father's brother's sons) and their sons and grandsons. When there were many sons in each generation, the group would be large.

Blood money

They called themselves the "one body" or "blood brothers". If a man was killed by someone from another group, any one of them could seek vengeance by killing any one of the other group. Instead, they could agree to accept "blood money" in compensation, and every one of the killer's group had to pay his share. The group owned a stretch of tribal territory and all the wells on it. They united to defend the territory against intruders.

The sheikh

Each group had its own headman or sheikh. He did not have great power because the Bedouin were very democratic. All major decisions were made after full discussions with the other men of his group. He had to have qualities of leadership, courage and wisdom to command their respect. He also had to be rich enough to entertain the group's guests; his tent was usually the largest. Wealth would also help him arrange good marriages for his sons and daughters which would increase his influence and power.

The sheikh was the spokesman for his group in all negotiations with other groups. Some would rise in importance to become the representative of the tribe, and would deal with the government of the country in which they lived.

A sheikh was usually succeeded by his eldest son. If the rest of the group did not think he had a suitable character, another would be chosen in his place. Often it was a younger brother of the sheikh or a cousin.

Summer camps

During the summer months, the Bedouin tents were concentrated near large wells. These gave water for them and their animals throughout the dry season. Camps were large, sometimes with as many as a hundred tents. The tents were pitched close together, but far enough away from the wells to allow large numbers of animals to be watered daily without upsetting camp life.

Only when the site became polluted were the tents moved. They were taken up and pitched a little distance away.

Spring camps

When winter arrived and the first rains began to fall, the move away from the big wells began and the large camps began to break up into smaller units. The spring camps comprised no more than five or six tents, as a rule, and were made up of small family groups. The flocks and herds were kept close to the tents. The kids and lambs needed protection at night from wolves, and the women had to do the milking. The pasture close by was quickly exhausted, so the camp sheikh decided when to move, and chose the new site. He always took the advice of the young men who went to scout for suitable places.

Right: This young man on horseback was the eldest son of a Libyan sheikh. His father was an old man and, in this case, the son had all the important qualities of leadership that he needed to take his father's place in due time.

Below: A diagram of a spring camp in Libya. The family tree shows the relationships of the families living in the tents. Sheikh Ibrahim's was the largest tent because he entertained the visitors to the camp. His widowed sister lived under his protection because she had no sons to look after her.

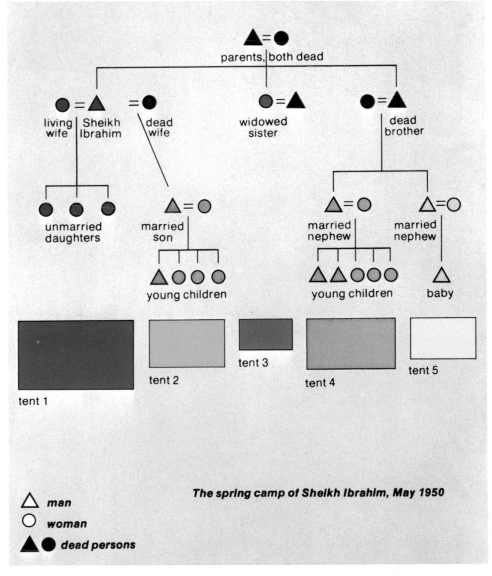

The spring camp of Sheikh Ibrahim, May 1950

△ man
○ woman
▲● dead persons

Hospitality

"O guest of ours though you have come, though you have visited us, though you have honoured our dwelling, we verily are the real guests, and you are the lord of this house."
A welcome from King Abdul Aziz al Saud to H.R.P. Dickson
The Bedouin host would say simply, *"This is your tent."*

The hospitality of the Bedouin is famous. No traveller in the desert could pass even the poorest tent without the owner rushing out and urging him to stop. It would be an insult to refuse. If no man were present, an older woman would come to offer hospitality in his place.

Desert travel was so dangerous that wayfarers had to know they could obtain food, drink and night's lodging at any tent they came across.

Some camps had special guest tents maintained by the whole community, but usually it was the sheikh who did the entertaining in his big tent.

Welcoming a guest
Strangers were never asked their identity or their business when they arrived. First there would be the long, elaborate ceremony of coffee or tea-making. Meanwhile words of welcome and greetings were exchanged, and enquiries about health made.

If the guest or guests looked important, an animal was sent for and slaughtered in their honour and a feast made. Sometimes the blood was smeared on the necks of their camels.

It was said that a poor man would slaughter his last animal for a guest, or if he had none, he could compel his neighbours to help him.

Sanctuary for three days
After the meal, the guests were always urged to stay for at least one night. When a guest ate his host's food, he was "eating his salt", and a special bond was created between them. The host was then bound to protect his guest for three days.

For invited guests lavish feasts were prepared. A reputation for hospitality was very important to a sheikh. The more people he entertained, the more favours he could claim in return.

Below: A Bedouin feast in Qatar. The meal prepared in the shade of the tent. The cloth laid on carpets spread out on the ground for the guests to sit on. It is an all-male occasion.

The feast is unusual by traditional Bedouin standards. In the past there would have been no cloth, and the selection of fresh fruits and of lettuces would not have been there. Nowadays they are freely available in the town markets. The large wooden bowl filled with rice, and the joints of meat piled up in the centre, are true to Bedouin tradition.

34

Below: This group of men and boys have just slaughtered an animal in preparation for a feast. They have skinned it and cut it into joints. These are now lying in a wooden bowl waiting for the women to take them away for cooking. Meanwhile the men rest from their labours over coffee.

Far left: The first stage in the elaborate coffee-making ceremony in Jordan. A man grinds up coffee beans using a brass mortar and pestle. Much has been written about "the pleasantest of all music in Bedouin ears – the ringing sound of pestle striking mortar in the process of pounding up coffee" (H.R.P. Dickson).

Left: When the coffee has been brewed on the fire, it is poured into the most splendid of the coffee pots, and then poured out by the host into little handleless coffee cups. Only a small amount is served at a time, but each guest may have several cups.

Religion

"There is no God but God (Allah), *and Mohammad is the prophet of God."*
The basis of the religion of Islam

Although the Bedouin knew little of the finer points of the teachings of Islam, they were very religious. Every activity was begun with the words "In the name of God". When asked how they were, they replied and said "Thanks be to God", and they declared their truthfulness by saying "By God".

The killing of an animal was seen as a sacrifice. Its throat was cut "in the name of God".

Islam

They knew the five pillars upon which Islam rests: the belief in one God; daily prayers; the giving of alms; the month of fasting from sunrise to sunset, and the pilgrimage to Mecca — and observed them as best they could.

Being illiterate, they could not read the Koran, the holy book of Islam, for themselves. Travelling teachers, *figis*, came round the camps and taught the boys to recite certain parts by heart. It was their only formal education.

Holy men were revered and their tombs became places of pilgrimage. Here oaths were sworn, and things of value left for safe-keeping.

Superstitions

Bedouin, especially the women, were also very superstitious. They greatly feared the curse of the "Evil Eye". Gazelle horn, cowrie shells, pearl buttons, blue beads and silver charms shaped like hands were used as charms against it.

Most powerful of all was the written name of God and other words from the Koran. The travelling *figis* would write for them on small pieces of paper, which were then sewn up into little leather purses and worn round the neck. Men, women, children, horses, camels and tents all carried such amulets.

Left: The grave of a holy man in Libya. Articles such as ploughs have been left there for safe keeping.

Right: 1, 2 Clothes worn by a boy for his circumcision. His mother drew a good luck sign on his shirt with henna, and tied scented beads onto his hat. **3** An amulet. **4** A baby's bonnet bearing charms against the Evil Eye.

Below: A Bedouin at prayer in the desert of Abu Dhabi. He faces in the direction of Mecca. Prayers are said five times every day.

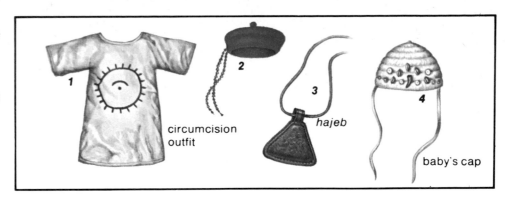

1

2

circumcision outfit

3

hajeb

4

baby's cap

Bedouin as warriors

"To despise wealth and to live from hand to mouth on booty captured by his own valour, after having squandered his patrimony in lavish hospitality, was the ideal of the Arabian cavalier."
Gerald du Gaury, in Arabian Journey

Before central governments in the Arab countries became strong, the Bedouin loved to go raiding. To them it was a sport, like hunting, which encouraged bravery, hardiness and skill.

They raided camps of rival groups, often hundreds of kilometres away, in order to capture camels. They relied on swift camel travel, and on taking the camp completely by surprise. Taking the camels from a rival group helped the raiders over a lean season. When their herds had built up, they would be raided in turn. There was very little bloodshed during these raids. If the men of the camp saw that they were hopelessly outnumbered they retired without putting up a fight, vowing to stage a return raid to retrieve their herds. The women and children were never harmed.

Tribal warfare

There were also frequent inter-tribal wars resulting from blood feuds. Bitter hatred arose when one tribal sheikh became so powerful that he wished to extend his power over others.

It was hard to unite tribes in large armies under a leader not of their own tribe, but it could be done when they were fighting a common enemy.

Lawrence of Arabia

This happened during the campaign of "Lawrence of Arabia" in World War I. The Turks were then the overlords of Arabia and Lawrence's mission was to advise the Arabs on how to conduct a revolt against them. The man chosen as leader of the army was not a tribal sheikh, but a member of a great religious family, son of the Sharif of Mecca. He had the qualities necessary in a war leader, and the tribesmen followed him gladly.

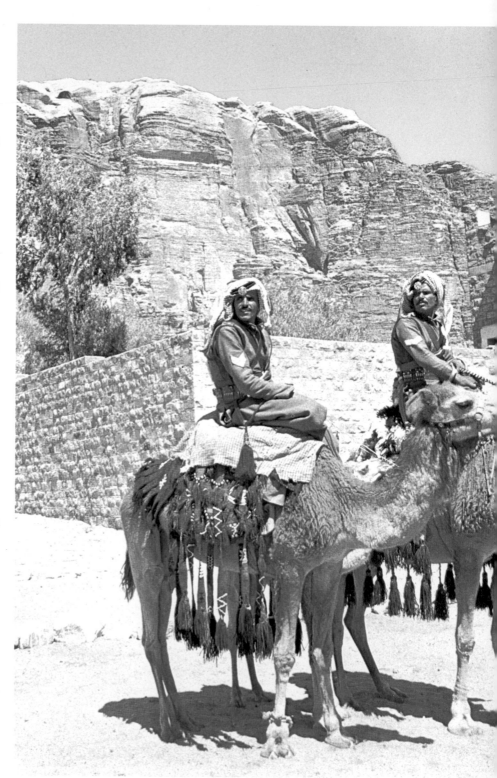

Left: Mounted soldiers of the Camel Corps, part of the army of King Hussein of Jordan. Bedouin did not take easily to the regimentation of regular army life, but the Camel Corps, originally built up and trained with the help of British officers, became a well disciplined fighting force.

Right: T.E. Lawrence meets with the Arab nationalist leaders of Baghdad and Damascus. Lawrence is on the right. Though a British Army officer, he wore Arab dress in Arabia, as it was more practical for the desert climate. It made camel riding far more comfortable than it was in army uniform trousers.

Below: A photograph taken from the collection of T. E. Lawrence – "Lawrence of Arabia". It shows the Bedouin army mounted on camels, following their leader, Prince Feisal, with banners flying. It was said of Lawrence by Robert Graves, "He based his strategy on an exhaustive study of the geography of his area; of the Turkish Army; of the nature of the Bedouin tribes and their distribution. So he based his desert tactics on a study of the raiding parties of the Arabs."

Oil in the desert

"The bright lights of the cities have lured away the sons of the Bedouin. What can the desert offer to compare with the refrigerator, the air-conditioner, the cinema and the Coca-Cola machine?"
William R. Polk, camel traveller

Below: An oil well in Kuwait, where production began in 1956. Before then it was a poor country with a small population making a meagre living from nomadic grazing and date growing. Today the population has increased over ten times, and it is the richest per head in the world.

The lives of the Bedouin have been greatly affected by the development of the oil industry in Arab lands. These countries had always been relatively poor in the past, but when oil was discovered and produced suddenly they became among the richest in the world.

Roads across the desert
The oil industry demanded new oil wells, and all the equipment needed had to be moved to the sites by road. With the money they received from exporting crude oil to the industrial nations, the Arab governments could build good roads from end to end of their countries, right across the desert. They imported cars, lorries and even aeroplanes and built airports near the major towns. The result was that camels were no longer essential.

Move to the towns
Camels had always been the Bedouin's greatest source of wealth. Suddenly the high price of riding camels fell; they were no longer needed for caravans of pilgrims or merchants crossing the deserts, or for army baggage trains.

At the same time, enormous sums of money were spent on finding new supplies of water. With the new drilling equipment to hand, deep wells were made, supplying water for irrigating dry parts of the desert. New fertile areas were created. Now that their traditional lifestyle was seriously threatened, many Bedouin were tempted to settle on the new farming land. Many of the young men found jobs with the oil companies.

The money from oil went on vast schemes to improve education, health services and housing. The Bedouin learned to accept these benefits and many became urban dwellers.

Below: Transporting camels in Saudi Arabia. After the discovery of oil, highways were built across the desert and motor transport introduced. Cars are quicker than camels, and lorries carry heavier loads.

Bottom of page: A Saudi Arabian farmer. Before the discovery of oil, little of Saudi Arabia was cultivated. Of that, most was in the oases. Since then the government has put into operation many projects for increasing water supplies, so much more land can be used.

The change from life in a tent to life in a house caused many difficulties for the Bedouin family, particularly for the women who had never left the desert before. Basic things had to be learned, such as how to use door handles, electric lights and toilets. They had to learn how to obtain water by turning on taps, and how to conserve it by turning them off!

The new house

Cooking methods in a house were so very different that many Bedouin women at first continued to cook in the old familiar way outside in the courtyard. Some Libyan Bedouin when first given houses pitched their tents alongside and used the houses for the animals. The houses were airless compared with the tents. Carpets and mats laid on sand were more comfortable and warmer than laid on concrete. If beds and chairs were bought their life style would be revolutionised. Cleaning a tent was easy; there was no rubbish to accumulate and all that was needed was a quick sweep with a dried shrub for a brush to keep the sand smooth. If the site became too dirty, it was easy to move. House cleaning involved far more drudgery.

A new way of life

The pattern of camp life with relatives living close together was destroyed when each family had its own house. Neighbours might not be related at all. The women were no longer able to come and go as they pleased, and with the men away at work they were forced to stay in their houses.

One Bedouin made this comparison: "In my tent I had an amulet hanging up containing words from the Koran; on my house I have a lightning conductor."

The way ahead

"Tomorrow is in the hands of God."
A favourite Bedouin saying

Below: A Bedouin resettlement house in Abu Dhabi, a sheikhdom on the Persian Gulf which has produced oil since 1963. Abu Dhabi city is on an island connected by causeway to the mainland, and many Bedouin have settled there, to work in the oil industry, bringing some animals with them.

Bottom of page: Sheikh Rashid of Dubai signs a contract for oil research on his land. Dubai is a tiny sheikhdom on the Persian Gulf, and its ruler granted rights for oil exploration in 1966. Production began in 1969.

No one can tell how long the oil of Arabia will last. The industrial countries of the world are still using it up at an alarming rate. The Organization of Petroleum Exporting Countries (OPEC), which includes the Arab countries, are making plans for the time when the precious oil supply runs out. There is exploration for other minerals, and development of industries while the oil revenue lasts, but nothing is likely to bring in the wealth that oil has.

The demand for water

The Arab states need more food and water in the new cities. Their population has greatly increased; the Bedouin have come into the towns seeking work, and thousands of technicians, traders and professional people have flocked in from elsewhere. Enormous quantities of water are needed for sanitation, washing and maintaining parks and gardens. Even more important, it is needed for irrigating the land to grow food.

More efficient drilling has increased the amount of water available from deep wells, but has caused the underground water table to fall alarmingly. In some areas sea water has been drawn in to replace the fresh water; a disaster for agriculture.

Water sources

New ideas for obtaining fresh water include tapping "fossil water", building dams to retain the rain from *wadis* after winter storms, and de-salinating sea water. All these schemes need money from the oil sales; if the oil fails, water could become scarce.

If this happened, would the Bedouin return to the desert? It is easy for the Bedouin to become settled, but it is almost impossible for settled people to become Bedouin.

Below: The first woman to be appointed inspector of schools in Qatar, another small state on the Persian Gulf made rich by oil. She symbolizes the increased educational opportunities for women as well as for men, and the freedom women now have there to wear western dress and go unveiled.

It might seem that in the oil-rich Arab states the significance of the Bedouin way of life in the desert is at an end. This is not, however, the whole story.

The amount of land suitable for growing plant foods has increased with the help of irrigation. There is more food available for the new town dwellers, but with their high standards of living they demand a new diet. They require daily supplies of meat; they are not content with the slaughter of animals only on special occasions. The religious importance of the animal sacrifice has largely been lost in the towns, although every slaughter must be performed in the proper Moslem way, accompanied by the words "In the name of God".

Rearing animals for meat

The new, expensively irrigated agricultural land cannot be used for the raising of animals for meat, a wasteful process in any case. This must be done in the semi-deserts, where grazing is free. There must still be nomadic herdsmen.

The market for riding and baggage camels has largely gone, but the demand for camel meat has greatly increased. This applies to mutton and lamb and, to a lesser extent, goat meat.

The problem of watering larger flocks and herds in the desert is solved by transporting barrels of water in lorries.

The new herders

Nowadays the nomadic herders in the desert are not family groups with their own animals, but paid herdsmen employed by merchants from the towns. They still need the old Bedouin knowledge and skills to survive in the desert, but their pattern of life is no longer the traditional one.

43

Things to do

Make a model of a Bedouin tent

First collect the materials: A base board or piece of cardboard painted a sandy colour. A piece of material for the tent top. This may be black if you wish to make an Arabian tent, or white with black stripes for a Saharan one. It should be about 25 cm×20 cm. String to make the tent ropes. Tape for making the braids which go over the tent poles. Pieces of wooden dowelling for the poles. You will need 2 poles 10 cm long, and 10 poles 5 cm long. Strips of material for the tent sides. Pins for attaching the sides to the tent top. Drawing pins or small nails to act as tent pegs for holding the ropes. Glue.

(1) First mark the central seam as shown. Then mark two lines at right angles dividing the top into three equal parts. Over these two lines stick pieces of tape. At the corners and along the sides where shown, firmly stick or sew loops of string. These are for holding the tent ropes. Loop the string for the tent ropes through these using slip knots (2). Each rope is about 25 cm long. Mark the positions for the poles.

Next turn your tent top over on the base board and put in one of the main tent poles. Fix the ropes on either side of it onto the board. Do not stretch them tightly at this stage. Do the same with the second tent pole, and then with the others, fixing down the ropes as you do so. If you now tighten the ropes by the slip knots, the tent should stand.

Pin the tent sides to the top. The front one may be left off altogether, or it may be partly pinned on, leaving an entrance at one side.

Make a dark circle in the front of the entrance to represent the fireplace and put in three little stones for

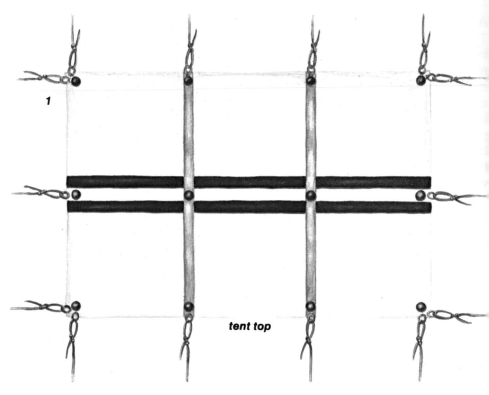

tent top

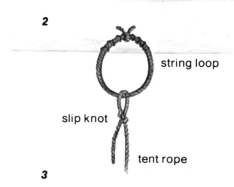

string loop

slip knot

tent rope

holding up the cooking pot (3). Put a bundle of dried moss or twigs nearby to look like the brushwood used on the fire.

If several people co-operate in making a number of tents, these can form a camp. You could also make people and animals for the camp.

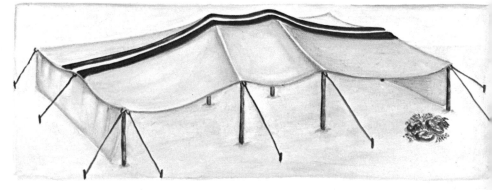

Amulet

This is a simple amulet made for a baby, to ward off the "Evil Eye". To make it, measure out a length of string by winding it round your wrist and middle finger as shown. Remove it, thread on four blue beads and a pearl button, and tie it back on your hand. You may need to ask a friend to help you when tying the string at the wrist.

Hajeb – a leather purse amulet

Cut out pieces of brown felt like the ones below. The Bedouin sew slips of paper inside with words from the Koran, but you can write a secret message if you prefer. Sew up the three long sides with running stitch, and catch in the ends of the "loop" at the top. The charm safely inside, you can hang the amulet round your neck or keep it somewhere special.

Silver amulet

The Bedouin use silver jewellery of many kinds. This one can be made from cardboard and silver paper. Cut out the shape with sharp scissors from cardboard. Rub silver paper with the end of a spoon until it's flat and shiny, and glue it onto the back and front of the card shape. Trim the edges. When it is dry, mark on the decorations with a penknife.

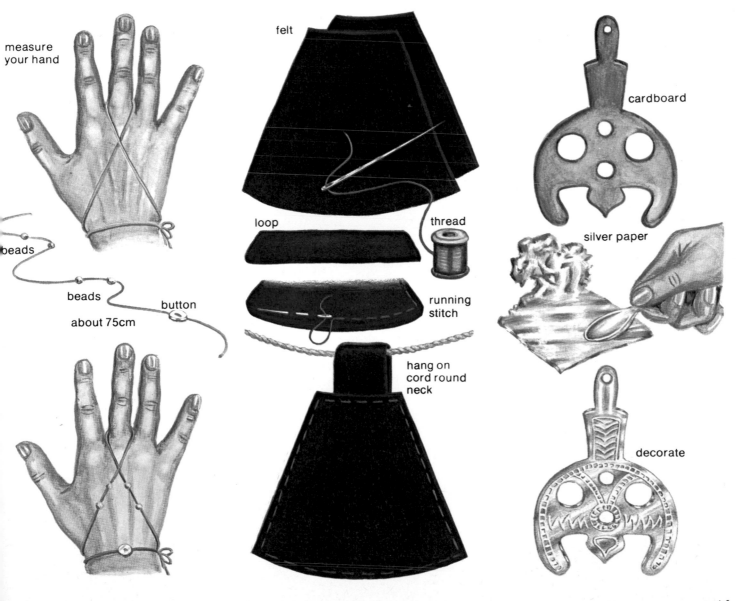

measure your hand

beads

beads

button

about 75cm

felt

loop

thread

running stitch

hang on cord round neck

cardboard

silver paper

decorate

Reference

The Arabic language

There are many dialects of Arabic spoken throughout the Arab world, but that spoken by the Bedouin is nearer to the classical Arabic, that is the Arabic in which the Koran is written, than any of the town dialects.

Although they could neither read nor write, the written words of the Koran were very important to them. One cure for illness was to have a *figi* write the name of God and other words from the Koran on the inside of a bowl with special ink, and the words were then washed off with water and drunk by the patient.

The special ink used for this was made by burning some sheep's wool until it was black, and then mixing it in water. This ink was also used for writing on the pieces of paper to be put inside the little leather purses.

Arabic writing goes from right to left, and their books begin at what we call the back.

Some Arabic words

this is the name of God.

these are the opening words of the Koran.
They mean, "In the name of God the merciful, the compassionate."

Some Arabic phrases much used by the Bedouin

Salām alaikum, peace be on you.
Alaikum as salām, on you be peace. This greeting and reply are used whenever people meet. (ā is long as in *ah*.)
Tafaḍal, literally means "honour" or "favour", as in "do me the honour"; it is used in phrases like "please come in", "please sit down", etc.
Allahi zīḍ fadlak, may God increase your favour or honour. This is said in reply to *Tafaḍal*.
Mun faḍlak, from your honour or favour. It means "if you please". (ḍ is pronounced *th* as in "the"; the *ī* is long as *ee*.)
Allahi kathir khairak, may God increase your wealth; used for "thank you".
Marhaba, welcome.

Bedouin seasons

Rabia, spring. This word can also mean "spring herbage". Spring is approximately February, March and April.
Saif, summer. This is May, June and July.
Kharif, autumn. This is August, September and October.
Shita, winter. This is November, December and January.

Some important dates

AD 570 The prophet Mohammad was born in Mecca.
622 Mohammad moved from Mecca to Medina. This became the first year of the Moslem calendar.
632 Mohammad died in Medina.
640–642 Egypt was conquered by the Arabs.
732 The Moslem Empire reached its fullest extent.
1051 The Bedouin tribes, Beni Hilal and Beni Sulaim, invaded the eastern Sahara. They were the ancestors of the Libyan Bedouin.
1503 Ludovico de Varthema became one of the first Christians to enter Mecca in disguise.
1869 The Suez Canal was opened for shipping. This stopped the free travel of Bedouin and of wild animals between the Saharan and Arabian deserts.
1875–76 Charles Doughty journeyed in Arabia and wrote of his impressions of the Bedouin.
1916–17 The Arab Revolt took place during World War I. The Arab army was made up chiefly of Bedouin and was advised by T. E. Lawrence.
1911–32 The Italian invasion and gradual conquest of Libya took place. The Bedouin fought a long guerrilla campaign against them, following religious leaders, the Sanussi.
1920 Oil first discovered in Iraq.
1935 King Ibn Saud granted the first oil rights in Saudi Arabia.
1943 The Italians were expelled from Libya by the Allies during the desert campaign of World War II.
1946–7 Wilfred Thesiger journeyed in Arabia and brought back much Bedouin lore.
1946 Oil production began in Kuwait.
1949 Oil production began in Qatar.
1959 Oil production began in Libya.
1960 Oil production began in Abu Dhabi.
1967 Oil production began in Oman.
1971 William R. Polk and William J. Mares crossed the Arabian desert and brought back a picture of the breakdown of the Bedouin way of life.

46

Book list

Few books have been written on the Bedouin for younger readers, but there is a great amount of literature for adults, some of which would certainly be enjoyed by older children. Both kinds are listed.

For younger readers:

A Closer Look at the Bedouin by Fidelity Lancaster (Hamish Hamilton).
The Bedouin by Shelagh Weir (World of Islam Festival Publishing Company).
The Desert by A. Starker Leopold (Time-Life International).
The Bedouin by Shirley Kay (David & Charles).

For adults and older readers:

Travels in Arabia Deserta by Charles M. Doughty (Jonathan Cape).
The Manners and Customs of the Rwala Bedouins by Alois Musil (American Geographical Society).
The Desert and the Sown by Gertrude Bell (Heinemann).
Arabian Journey and other desert travels by Gerald de Gaury (George G. Harrap & Company Limited).
Seven Pillars of Wisdom by T. E. Lawrence (Jonathan Cape).
The Arab of the Desert by H. R. P. Dickson (Allen & Unwin).
Sons of Ishmael by G. W. Murray (Routledge & Sons Limited).
Travellers in Arabia by Robin Bedwell (Hamlyn).
Passing Brave by William R. Polk and William J. Mares (Knopf, New York).
The Golden Ode by William R. Polk (University of Chicago Press).
Arabian Sands by Wilfred Thesiger (Longman).

Glossary

Aromatic. Having an aroma, or spicy fragrance.
Arranged marriage. One where the parents decide whom the child shall marry.
Blood feud. A feud between kin groups arising from an act of bloodshed.
Blood money. Compensation paid to the kin group of someone killed.
Broth. A thin soup.
Chevron. A V-shaped pattern.
Cistern. A natural reservoir of water.
Clarified butter. Butter that has been heated and skimmed to remove impurities and help it keep longer. In Indian cooking it is called *ghee*. It is very useful in hot climates where there are no refrigerators.
Evil Eye. A powerful look which some believe causes harm.
Fellahin. Settled Arab farmers.
Figi. A wandering teacher of Islam.
Guerrilla warfare. Informal warfare waged by small bands of well-concealed fighters, usually against a larger, more structured army.
Henna. A powder made from a plant which makes a red dye when mixed with water and heated.
Herbage. Greenery, especially grass.
Khol. A dark brown or black powdery colouring used as a natural cosmetic.
Moslem. A member of the Islamic faith.
Nomad. A wanderer with no settled home.
Peninsula. A piece of land surrounded by water on three sides. It means "almost-island".
Pilgrimage. A journey to a holy place.
Revere. Honour, have deep respect for.
Sanctuary. A safe place where you are protected from enemies.
Semi-desert. An area with very little rainfall, but where some plants grow for at least part of the year.
Spindle. A spinning stick used to wind a woollen thread round.
Stimulant. An item of food or drink which "keeps you going" when the body is tired.
Tattoo. Marks on the face and body thought to increase beauty. Bedouin tattoos were pricked into the skin with a needle dipped in blue dye.
Trilling. A high-pitched noise made by wagging the tongue rapidly to and fro. It was done by women to express joy.
Utensil. A useful tool or vessel, especially one used in cookery.
Wadi. A valley where rain water runs off desert hills.
Wayfarer. A traveller.
Wedding settlement. An agreed amount of money or gifts paid to the family of a bride by the groom's family.

Index

48